inside, outside, and everything in between

Sophia Li

BookLeaf
Publishing

India | USA | UK

inside, outside, and everything in between ©
2022 Sophia Li

All rights reserved.

No part of this publication may be
reproduced, stored in a retrieval system, or
transmitted, in any form or by any means,
electronic, mechanical, photocopying,
recording or otherwise, without the prior
written permission of the presenters.

Sophia Li asserts the moral right to be
identified as author of this work.

Presentation by *BookLeaf Publishing*

Web: www.bookleafpub.com

E-mail: info@bookleafpub.com

ISBN: 9789357448444

First edition 2022

DEDICATION

to past-me, present-me, and future-me: this is a chapter of your life. treasure it.

to my parents: thank you for everything.

to my friends: I am okay, don't worry:)

ACKNOWLEDGEMENT

There are many people I should acknowledge, but I most definitely have to acknowledge my creative writing teacher for encouraging me onward, challenging me to do better and harder things, to test the limits of what I can do and fall bravely into the unknown. Thank you, Ms Carol, for facilitating my growth as a writer. You unknowingly made this journey so much easier and so much harder at the same time. I couldn't be more grateful.

PREFACE

There is very little to say about this, except that it is pieces of me, jumbled together, a bedazzling mosaic of everything I am, everything I think, and then some. It is deeply personal and observational, knots of words I vomited onto a page in order to think more clearly, or descriptions of the natural world to distract my mind. This is my first book, and I acknowledge that I am young. I'm floundering in the dark, feeling along the walls.
Some parts of the book might not be pretty to read, but maybe that's the whole point. Humans aren't always pretty creatures, and I think this might represent that, at least a little.

caliginosity: lack of light

take a breath
deep dive
white bubbles
marred vision   there's no light
i cannot see

i touch my mind
my heart
feel its pulsations
ripple through me
foreignness
i don't understand me

inside: wondering

the sun crawls across
the arc of the sky
drags heat and light with it
and leaves me
wondering
am i okay…?
it's hard to tell
i can't think about
it, for too long
it's like staring
into the sun

i sit as i think, brushing
worries out of my hair
they pile on the hardwood floor

i sweep them away
out of fear of
uncleanliness

inside: invalidation

I feel like a fraud
very often
surface water issues
dramatized thoughts
my brain considers them
invalid

I don't know
what's real and what's not
I don't know if I'm okay
or not

all I know
is that there is something
a festering disease
or maybe an invisible wound
will it be cured?
will it heal?
or will it infect
leave me to rot?

inside: un-useful math

i know how to solve
for y in math
sometimes, you can
substitute in x
but there's no
x
i can substitute into
the equation of my feelings
to discover
(wh)y
i feel this way sometimes

inside: underneath

i went sailing
today, gliding
over velvet water
sparkling like
a handful of
diamonds
under sunlight and a cloudless sky
the boat rocks
left
    right
left
    right
the waves roll, ripple
unseen things thrash under

like my mind
i never know what's

underneath

inside: masochism?

maybe I'm a masochist

I have a habit
of inviting out the darkness
to sit by my side
when no one else will

the same darkness
that could turn on me in a heartbeat
disassemble everything I am
insert doubt into my mind
and leech my self confidence

yet I still invite it
coax it forwards
voluntarily
pick it up
feel its deceptive softness

I turn it over
examine it
fingers probing
for the sharp edges
I know are hidden, waiting

and
prick

regret d
            r
              i
                p
                  s
                        like blood

but I don't learn

(maybe because I don't want to)

inside: taste of mediocrity

I think I'm okay
emphasis on "think"
because I don't know what okay tastes like

is it sweet like brown sugar boba?
    is it floral like rose water, sipped on a beach?
        is it refreshing like an alcohol-free piña
colada?

somebody tell me
because I don't know

inside: mold or coffin?

there is a mold I've created for myself
unfitting
loose like baggy clothes
on a thin frame
tight like a rope-noose
or metal shackles

it constricts my chest
squeezes my lungs
and my breaths
uneven, erratic

inhale
exhale
in-
ex-

oxygen retreats
from my windpipe

i can't breathe

maybe it's a coffin

inside: inky escape;
garbage mind

I dive into books
as an escape
i'm beginning to realize

In the spaces
of inked words, square letters
on a whispering page

I find my company,
understanding,
in the shape
of a Latin alphabet
riddled page
filled with neat
squid ink colored words

I say them out loud
roll the shape of the words
around in my mouth
chewing on
vowels

consonants
and
emotions

Like something I can swallow
consume
to feel fuller
less. . .
void
less like a shell
echoing of the ocean

I guess
that's my life
gorging myself
on others' writing
feeling horrible about my own
swimming in pages
oxygen in chapter breaks
drowning the doubt
self-reproach like debris

our minds, vehicles
carting around
useless junk
truck loads of trash
diseases festering
insecurities like flies

my mind is infected
plagued by worries
and while you may assure me
my writing is fine

will my mind believe you?

outside: different perspectives

i don't always understand
the turbulence within me
so I sit
look outside
watch the turbulence of the sea
instead
if I can't stare at the sun
then I can at least
watch the cumulus clouds
white and grey seagulls
navy-turquoise water
the world the sun
travels through
I watch, observe
imagine

imagining outside: paradox of loneliness

a male deer walks slowly
proudly, down a slope
rich with grass, overgrown
stalks for his leisure feasting
he has had a lonely day
fraught with silences and non-silences
flies nagged in his ears
one landed on his antlers
and when he shooed them off
he missed their
voices

so he bites into the sun
and drags it with him
for company

imagining outside: in a bathing suit, dancing through time

In a bathing suit, 4
intimidated by royal blue
seeking asylum in a mother's embrace
from the foamy tips —
it's a one way trip
lapping at ankles; cold, wet kisses on skin
I wasn't a big fan of its vast expanses and gilded
surface.

In a bathing suit, 6
treading a carpet of fallen stars
as they shine like sprinkled glitter
gold and bold, bracketing a turquoise sea

Stars in a jar, I take home with me

In a bathing suit, 8
foreign waters of a foreign country

red octopus on land
green sea serpent buried in sand
a sun hopeful over the horizon
an aqua blue liquid gem,
refracting
reflecting

shards in a jar, I take home with me,
eroded edges in red, green, blue, white.

In a bathing suit, now
I stand by the shore
feeling
the biting, crisp cold
pebbles dig into skin
memories swell, crest, roll
kissing the shoreline
goodbye

imagining outside:
flaking autumn
memories

Night nudges day away
pulling the curtains on the world
and the city lights
like fireflies, like amber fossils
trapped in the inky lake

Jeweled leaves
on the arbutus trees
that line the sidewalk
rustle like windy fingers through hair
as paper-thin bark
flakes, peels
crumbles,
like cookies,
like childhood,
like memories.

Autumn is frail.

imagining outside:
the rain

Sometimes I liken the rain to tears
fat droplets, trailing down her blue dome cheeks
rolling, rolling, rolling
from under cloudy eyelashes

And sometimes, I sit under the rain
breathe in the unique smell of it
the way freshness overwhelms my nostrils
on each inhale

I wonder at rain, sometimes,
and I've come to the conclusion that it is
necessary
a deep cleanse
to de-clutter, to let go

And I wonder if the sky is ashamed
of her crescendoing thunder
her brutal lightning
the rain she unleashes

If even she, the one who holds up our world

And lets herself brim with light, for our sakes
feels afraid
feels angry
feels sad
feels lonely

she must, I've concluded
sitting under the rain
bathing in this peace she offers
at the expense of her pain

so if I can find this form of catharsis —
this necessary process she undergoes;
this sacrifice she makes;
to keep us healthy and thriving —
so calming, so healing

then why are we so afraid of our tears
so ashamed of something
that was designed to bring us
the relief we all need
for a healthier living?

outside:
blow-torched sky

At the onset of evening
the seas are paintings
brushstrokes of lights and darks
reflections running
like watercolour

As overhead
the skies burn, melt

erode the horizon

outside: yolk moon

graphite sky
smudges of clouds
a yolk gold moon
leans over the
horizon

and sets the water
on fire

cars roll to halt
slack jawed passengers
climb out hypnotically
cell phones raised
cameras clicking

how often does
one see a gold
moon?
rarely

unique, proud
it owns the sky
like a second sun

so bask in your
exceptionality
and make the crowd
gasp

everything in between: snapshot of home

turquoise bowl, sunset-
oranges, wrinkled skin
pink clouded peaches

picture shot
in-between frame
a white-brown ragdoll cat
shoves her face into
the flower stems arranged
in a brown vase

she might be enjoying
the scent of the flowers
or maybe
she's just a
terrible model

i love her immensely

everything in between: library of memories

rewalking
the library of my memories
I come across
a tome titled
paris

its pages are thin
ink running together
but one entry remains clear

the eiffel tower at night
had gold dripping down its sides
like melted wax

I remember
squeezing onto
a creaky elevator

stepping out into
velvet ink

so remote
as paris shimmered underneath us

in that moment
it felt like
I could reach up a hand
brush the stars
and pull back fingers
with glittery residue
a stamp of experience
a seal of presence

that says
look, I've been here

brilliance:
brightness of light

i haven't written fractured poems like the
'insides' in a while

i used to touch my heart
whisper
bleed, dear heart
bleed, so i can
dip my finger in the ruby
write with blood

i used to dig my fingers   under my rib cage
pry it open, peek inside
disassemble myself
so i can reassemble
through writing

and when that red ink dried
when my rib cage slammed shut
i despaired   for in my mind
i'd lost inspiration

but   isn't that good?

maybe it's just
getting better
maybe i've finally   understood myself
my inner workings
less labyrinthine
less alien
maybe i've finally
begun figuring myself out

there is a sliver of brilliance now

thank you

dear reader

i want to begin
by thanking you
for walking through my mind
guided by this pair of hands   with fingers
that cannot reach
farther beyond a 9th on a piano

thank you, reader
for your courage
to step inside my head
listen to my senseless thoughts
and come through the other side

if you're still here,
thank you for staying
thank you for listening
thank you for accepting
the bits of brokenness   within me
i'm slowly mending

dear reader
i know that this wasn't
the most cohesive

that it was disjointed
hairline fractures between topics

but you stayed
despite everything
thank you so much

www.ingramcontent.com/pod-product-compliance
Lightning Source LLC
LaVergne TN
LVHW010946200726

843509LV00013B/2298